Our Nec

Pipe

Dreams

Wilderness Hunting Stories
of the Pacific Northwest

SANDY CATHCART

NEEDLE ROCK
PRESS

Visit Needle Rock Press at www.needlerockpress.com

www.sandycathcart.com

www.needlerockpress.com

Find Sandy Cathcart and Needle Rock Press on Facebook.

Our Neck of the Woods: Pipe Dreams

Copyright © 2019 Sandy Cathcart

Cover and inside photos by Sandy Cathcart. Copyright © 2019 by Sandy Cathcart.

Needle Rock Press
341 Flounce Rock Rd.
Prospect, OR 97536

Some Needle Rock Press books may be purchased in bulk at reduced rates. For information, please email sandy@sandycathcartauthor.com

ISBN-10: 1-943500-14-2
ISBN-13: 978-1-943500-14-7 (Needle Rock Press)

DEDICATION

To Steve Evans
the toughest outdoorsman
I have ever known
and
my very best "girlfriend"

Steve Evans on Gopher Ridge Trail

About This Book

FOR OVER TWENTY YEARS, starting in the early nineties, I interviewed oldtimers, listened to hundreds of hunting stories, and experienced my own adventures in the wilds of the Upper Rogue Unit of Southern Oregon.

In 1996, I began sharing these stories in the pages of *Oregon Fish & Wildlife Journal*. Thank you, Cristy Rein, for seeing the value in these pieces of history!

Now, you are holding the first in several compilations. I hope you will enjoy these stories as much as I do. This first volume focuses on hunting in the Upper Rogue

Whether you have been a visitor here, lived for years here, or just been curious about our way of living that mirrors the old days, here is a piece of history to be relived and cherished for generations to come.

Many of the people mentioned in this volume have "walked on" from this world, but we still hold these men and women in our hearts. I can't help but think of them every time I step foot in the outdoors, which for me is every day.

Welcome to a walk through our neck of the woods!

Contents

Eddie LaFerriere near McKie Camp

Steve Evans

New Breed of Mountain Men

MOUNTAIN MEN HAVE LONG FOUND A HOME in our neck of the woods. As I look at 2008 still at the beginning of a new century, I am grateful to have known these rangy, bearded creatures with piercing eyes. I've known oldtimers who lived off the land and spurned society. They longed for adventure and found it and so much more in the highlands far from civilization.

Some folks think these men are gone, but I know better. I know a new breed of mountain men who live on the fringe and look for every opportunity to escape into wildness. They peer into sprawling forests and see a mystical land begging for adventure. They carry rifles, yet seldom use them, trusting instinct to know when to make a kill, very much like the other predators in the forest who roam the land for food.

1

They stand on far-seeing places with the wind in their faces pulling memories into a heart swollen fat with courage. They sleep in tents and warm themselves over pine-scented fires. Rain never deters them; snow brings a welcoming blanket of pure silence; storms merely spring them into action as they brace themselves and their gear for every possibility.

This year I watched as the mountain men I have long learned to love sprang into action. Wind roared through the canyon at Bessie Shelter, uprooting enormous trees with abandon and crashing them to the ground. A giant fir landed mere feet from a hunter's tent; another blocked the road, yet another barely missed one of the mules. The roar of the storm deafened our ears and the chill of it broke into our bones.

My job was to stand watch and holler if the biggest tree finally gave way to twisting agony and started falling toward the cook tent. Several times it groaned and creaked, and I feared for the brave men who fought against a force much larger than themselves.

Steve Evans, our hunting boss and maker of the tents, kept his ever-present smile in spite of a hunting trip cut short, ruined canvas, and a mess of a pack-up job. He was simply glad they were all alive and hoping they would remain so. The Cat Man and his brother, Dale, chased down errant canvas and flying cookery, never once looking toward the tree I was in charge of keeping watch over.

Eddie LaFerriere, our wrangler, looked more alive than ever as the wind turned his hair into a wild mass of energy. The thrill of the storm caught hold of my heart as I realized these men trusted me with their lives and loved me enough to keep me out of danger.

I'm glad for these men; thankful they have wormed their way into my life. Though they appear rough and rangy with their wild hair and even wilder eyes, I fear no harm from them or the storm.

In the 1800's Isabella Bird discovered the same kind of acceptance with a much-feared mountain man in the Rocky Mountains of Colorado. His name was Jim Nugent. She described him as a broad thickset man, about forty-five, who must have been strikingly handsome at one time in his life. But now one eye was entirely gone (lost in a bear attack), and the loss made one side of his face repulsive, while an artist might have modeled the other in marble. She said that "Desperado" was written in large letters all over him.

Isabella hired Mr. Nugent (she never called him Jim) as a guide to climb 14,700-foot Long's Peak, the last 500 feet of which were a perpendicular crawl up smooth pink granite. Dressed in a skirt and boots, Isabella nearly didn't make it, but Mr. Nugent took a rope and wrapped one end around her and another around himself and half dragged her up the mountain like a bale of goods.

Isabella said the view at the top was one that took her breath away and satisfied her soul.

That night Isabella discovered Mr. Nugent, the unlikely lone mountain man, felt the same way. He tearfully talked of his wayward life until she nearly thought love was possible. He was certainly hoping so. But she came to her senses realizing the life of a mountain man in 1873 would do nothing but drag her down. Mr. Nugent loved his alcohol far too well and lived a reckless life.

"He is a man," she said, "whom any woman might love but whom no sane woman would marry."

It was a sad end for Mr. Nugent as a well-aimed bullet killed him the following year. Perhaps it was a fitting end for a man who said he was so attached to Isabella that it was killing him.

Today's mountain men often face the same challenge in finding a woman who will love the land as much as they do. Sometimes it works out, like with The Cat Man and me and a handful of other couples we've known over the years. Yet more often it's a balancing act, with the woman attempting to change the man into something more civil while the man fights the call that burns deep in his soul.

Hunting camp is an answer to the mountain man caught between two worlds. For a few weeks each year, he can break free, grow a beard, drink strong whisky, and spin tall tales with abandon. He tromps through the forest with more imagination than reality and sleeps hard each night after spending so much energy. Then he returns home, clean-shaven and civil, abandoning his mountain love for the sweetheart who stole the greater part.

I feel for this new breed of mountain man who has but a few weeks per year to follow his heart, yet I'm glad he has the opportunity for at least this much.

So, as we look at 2008, having weathered every storm 2007 sent our way (and there were plenty of them), I thank The Creator once again for a year of wildness with a mountain man who has totally captured my heart. The Cat Man is the real thing, and I'm glad society has failed to change him. He's not alone in our neck of the woods where mountain men continue to thrive into a new century.

The Cat Man with His Cat, while Red Dog
Watches from a Distance

The Cat Man Gets His Cat

ASK ANYONE IN OUR NECK OF THE WOODS and they'll tell you it's important to listen to the oldtimers. When it comes to knowledge about the wilderness, these toughened men and women know what they're talking about.

I've learned from Wayne Marshall to never enter the wilderness without carrying a coat and emergency supplies, no matter what time of year, or how hot the weather, or how short my expected trip. Jack Hollenbeak taught me that it's important to stay alert, listen for every sound, and catch every movement, no matter how small. Archie McKillip cautioned that when someone says, "Run," you don't turn and look, you just do it. Nelson Nye passed on the good information that you should always let someone know where you're heading, no matter how secret the destination. Marvin Wright was adamant that when you take a rest in cougar country, you keep your back against a tree.

Every piece of information has been a lifesaver.

On a recent photo trip to Wildlife Images outside of Merlin in Southern Oregon, I applied the information Jack Hollenbeak gave me to stay alert, listen, and catch every movement.

The staff at Wildlife Images does an admirable job of preparing these injured and mistreated animals for a return trip to the wild, but some animals have been too domesticated by the time they arrive at the shelter. It's exciting to watch wolves, bears, lynx, and cougar, and it's easy to think they're perfectly harmless, but that is not the case. A wise viewer will always exercise a certain amount of caution.

One caution I missed before my first photo shoot was to not wear a hat. I discovered one of the reasons when I reached the cougar cage. Every time the big cat laid eyes on me, he would hold my gaze with an extreme intensity while his muscles tensed, and he slowly raised his body in my direction.

I would sneak to a different place, but he would soon discover me midst the crowd and give the same reaction every time.

Clark

I couldn't discern whether he was simply interested in me or if I reminded him of a long-held grudge he needed to make even. I was very glad of the strong wire between us.

On my second photo shoot, the cougar made the cutest little purring sound whenever he wanted the trainer to throw him something to eat. I'd never heard a cougar purr like that in the wild.

The most common sound I've heard them make is an otherworldly scream that causes everything in the forest to freeze and go silent with fear. After returning home, I told The Cat Man how impossible it seemed that an animal that makes such a cute little purr could be so dangerous.

Yet dangerous is a good word to use when describing cougars. In my research for former articles, I've talked with wildlife officials in seven different states, and by the time they finished their stories of cougar attacks, it took me a while to gain enough courage to solo hike back into the wilderness.

Turned out it was a good thing I told the Cat Man about that cute little purring sound.

On the second day of elk season, he guided his hunter, Mike Severini, up a steep face of mountainside where they both took a needed rest.

Of course, The Cat Man used oldtimer Marvin Wright's advice about keeping his back against a tree wider than his shoulders. He had Mike do the same. Mike leaned his rifle against the tree and stared downhill while The Cat Man readied to call. The wind was in his face, so he kept his vision downhill waiting for a coveted six-point bull to arrive. Mike waited too, finding himself getting a bit sleepy and thinking not much was gonna happen.

The Cat Man cow-called twice and heard a tiny mew behind him. It didn't sound right, but he didn't want to move until he was sure of what he was hearing. He decided to call again, but before he did, he heard another mew. This time, he peeked around the tree.

Less than twenty feet away, a cougar crouched on a rock, ready to spring.

Since Cat was guiding and not hunting, he didn't carry a rifle, but his reaction was quick. He swept his .44 revolver out of his holster and aimed. Pulling the hammer back, he heard something he had never heard before—an empty *Click*. He pulled again. *Click*. The third time, the revolver finally went bang and kicked up dirt beneath the cougar's feet.

Still, the cougar remained in a crouched position, every muscle ready to leap

Cat aimed again, *Click.*

The cougar sprang just as Cat pulled the fifth and final shot.

The bullet hit its mark just before the cougar did a backflip and came out running down the hill right between The Cat Man and Mike. Cat could have reached out and touched it on its way.

Meanwhile, Mike had risen to his feet to see what The Cat Man was shooting at. What he saw made him freeze in place. The cougar was headed directly at him.

"Ohhhhhhhhh shhhh…."

That's all he got out. The cougar did a side turn directly in front of Mike before disappearing into the bushes.

Later, when the guys told the story back at camp, Mike signed up for next year's trip, saying he had never seen anyone as cool as The Cat Man in the face of sudden danger.

"The guy stayed completely calm," Mike said, shaking his head. "I never even grabbed my rifle."

When they brought the body of the cougar out of the wilderness, a young surveyor called to them from the open window of his truck. He wanted an interview so he could fill out his report. The first question he asked was regarding the accommodations.

Mike and The Cat Man looked at each other. What accommodations? They had just come out of the wilderness where the only accommodations were the hard ground and a canopy of trees. But they simply shrugged.

Then the surveyor saw the cougar. "Where did you get that?" he asked.

Mike told the story, embellishing it more than just a bit. The surveyor wrote quickly while rolling his window up until there was only a small crack to speak through. By the time Mike told him about the bear that had come into camp the night before, the surveyor had had enough. He dropped his pad and pen and sped away making a cloud of dust behind him.

That night at camp, Cat added his own piece of advice to the oldtimers' list. "Make sure your pistol is clean and ready at all times, especially each night after crawling through the wilderness in increment weather."

Steve Evans, our outfitting boss, took photos of The Cat Man with his cat. It's one of the few times I've ever seen Cat smile for a photo. He had good reason. It's not often a younger man in our neck of the woods can join the ranks of the oldtimers by facing danger and meeting it head on with such wisdom and calm control. Seems like that's the way of it with the oldtimers good advice. It most often comes from making a bad mistake.

I can't help but wonder, though, if my little piece of information was some sort of God thing. Would Cat have turned in time if he hadn't recognized that cute little purring sound?

I'm thankful The Cat Man got his cat, especially before the cat got him.

Mike Severini, The Cat Man,
and Robert Garcia with the Cat

Sheltered from the Storm

Running With the Herd

AS A CHILD, I believed animals could understand me. I once talked to a coyote that stood a mere six feet from me. His ears were cocked in curiosity, but his body was poised to run. When I told him how beautiful he was, the tension seemed to leave him like ground fog vanishing in the morning sun.

That was a long time ago when I roamed our little northern California ranch with BB gun always in hand, ready to fend off the countless rattlesnakes sunning themselves on rocky hillsides (though I never actually shot one). Somewhere in the process of becoming an adult, I stopped talking to wild animals. But a recent experience kind of makes me wonder . . .

On a warmer-than usual winter morning, I stepped outside as the first rays of sun crossed the ridge over Flounce Rock.

A small movement in the trees caught my attention. Curious, and still dressed in nightshirt and slippers, I sneaked into the forest. A rust-orange rump appeared first, then the dark brown cape of an elk. *Beautiful.* A huge cow elk pulled at the bark high on a cedar while another nibbled at something interesting on the ground. A young bull pulled on an oak branch, suddenly breaking it off with a loud crack. As I continued staring, I could make out at least thirty elk drifting through the trees.

Wanting to get a better look, I edged closer. The herd had remained calm when the bull ripped down an entire branch, but when I merely snapped a twig, the lead cow shot up the hill with the others close behind.

Darn, I thought. *Now, they're gone.*

But the herd stopped and turned wary eyes back on me. I willed myself not to breathe or move, then I heard a snort from behind. Soon thirty elk became fifty. And I was right in the middle.

I waited in silence as the animals moved around me in their graceful, boat-like rhythm. A young bull came so close I could have reached out and touched him. When these new elk trailed the rest of the herd up the hill, I followed as quietly as possible, stepping carefully, heel-toe, on moss-covered rocks, stopping when the herd stopped, moving when they crossed a small ridge. Then I hurried a bit and a calf squealed, sending the whole herd running through a forest so thick I could only see a few feet ahead.

Consumed by a desire to follow, I searched for elk tracks in the moist earth and listened for their familiar sounds. For long minutes, silence shrouded the forest. Then a strange thing happened. It was like being in a great crowd of people where talk and laughter meld into a humming din, then suddenly each individual conversation becomes clear. I could hear water falling over stones, a woodpecker hammering on a faraway tree, the swoosh of a crow's wings, a gentle mew, then the clicking of hooves turning over rocks and snapping dry branches and thudding hollowly on bare ground. Through the trees, I could make out the outline of more than thirty rumps and the flickering of several pairs of ears. I marveled at how easy it would be to walk right past and never see an elk.

The lead cow gazed down at me from her perch on the highest ridge. The stare-down continued so long I began questioning what I was seeing. *Perhaps it's really a bush or rock. Surely an elk couldn't stand still for so long.* Just as I was about to move, the cow seemed to relax and turned her head to feed on oak leaves. Maybe she sensed I meant no harm.

Being accepted by her, however reluctantly, was exhilarating. But nothing surpassed what I felt as the herd moved around me, encircling me in its midst. Together we moved from the cover of the forest into the open meadow. As the elk spread out in the tall grass, they looked as though they had always been there, these majestic animals, so huge and yet so graceful.

For those few hours when I joined the elk herd as they rummaged for food beneath the shelter of Flounce Rock, I completely forgot myself and the pressures of living in the nineties.

For years, I had listened to my husband and father tell stories of the beauty and grace and excitement of the hunt. My romp with the elk herd gave me a taste of what those stories sought to share and, for the first time in my life, I felt a strong desire to take part in the hunt.

After months of diligent preparation, I set out on a blustery November morning. The snow swirled in little funnels as I scrambled over the rocks of Skookum Creek. I had traded my nightshirt for full winter gear, and I carried a rifle and backpack as I started my ascent up the mountain. My breathing seemed to echo like thunder through the quiet of the forest. Gray squirrels and Steller's jays served as sentinels, alerting the elk of approaching danger. More than once, the noisy critters made me abandon a good hiding spot.

Searching for the outline of familiar rumps while I followed their fresh tracks in the snow, I dreamed of a bull. My heart zoomed as I caught the musky aroma of a recent wallow, but the majestic animals stayed out of sight. I imagined the elk watching me, laughing at me, upholding their well-earned reputation as masters of elusion.

Each day, I arose well before dawn and followed the elk, returning in darkness to the warmth of home. Though weary from miles of hiking, I never once felt stressed. Fresh air renewed my senses, making me aware of the smallest pleasures; tiny purple flowers poking their heads through a thin layer of snow; the excitement of clouds suddenly parting to reveal a spectacular view; the gentle touch of a high-country breeze as it cooled my flushed cheeks. I was younger and more alive than I had been in years.

On the last day of the season, I hiked to the wilderness trailhead to meet The Cat Man on his return from guiding a hunt. No snow had fallen on this lower section of mountains. A sparkling stream gurgled through the meadow where I sat with my back against a warm rock. With rifle across my lap, I waited, idly hoping a bull elk would appear before my husband returned.

I had almost dozed off when the music of a thousand wind chimes filled the air. I sat up in wonder, realizing it was the wind blowing through the tops of fir trees. Thousands of seed pods swirled across the meadow, tinkling in the wind. As my eyes followed their flight, some landed on the soft brown face of a lone cow elk as she emerged from the forest. We became aware of each other at the same time.

Neither of us moved. My rifle lay across my lap. There was no need for it, for no bull joined her side. I wouldn't have taken aim even if one did. I was too entranced with the magic of the moment, too overcome with the awe I first felt on the day I ran with the herd.

A gray squirrel suddenly chattered a warning and, moments later, my husband and his crew came into view. With one bound the cow disappeared into the forest.

Slowly, I rose to meet The Cat Man.

Two beautiful racks graced the backs of the pack mules. After greeting me with a kiss, Cat asked if I had enjoyed a successful hunt.

"Yes," I answered.

His eyes grew large, "You got one?"

"No," I confessed, "But I had a great time."

He laughed and began unloading the pack team.

When I was sure no one was watching, I turned back to the meadow where I had last seen the cow and whispered, "See you later."

Perhaps I had reverted to my childhood self, talking with an animal like that, but it seemed the right thing to do.

So don't be surprised if you're walking in our neck of the woods and you discover someone talking to no one at all. Simply give them their space, because they've connected with a critter you cannot yet see. Give yourself enough time romping through our woods and who knows? Maybe next time you'll be the one running with the herd.

A Beautiful Bull Wapiti

23

Randy Roth and his
Magnificent Bear

In the Company of Nimrod

HUNTERS IN OUR NECK OF THE WOODS share a strong camaraderie. It binds us together even when we're heading alone off trail and enjoying the fresh scent of rain mingling with incense cedar. Out of season we spend our time planning and scouting through blazing heat, mud, or snow.

In season we scramble to free enough time to search the woods for the big one. Most of us never find it, or if we do, it's the wrong animal, or the wrong season, or both. Whether or not we are successful at finding the big one, we always enjoy the camaraderie of sharing enhanced stories as we hunker around crackling campfires.

Oldtimer's stories are as much about the one that got away as they are about the one they brought home. Even the successful old-time hunters like Nelson Nye, Archie McKillip and Jack Hollenbeak admitted to being skunked more often than not. From them, I've learned to tell folks that I'm a good hunter. Then after a brief pause, I say, "But I don't always find what I'm hunting for."

I laugh about the bull elk that strutted across the open field in front of me the last evening of deer season, and the five-point buck I ran into during . . . you guessed it . . . elk season. Happens to me all the time. But that's not what happens to Randy Roth. In him, I've discovered a true nimrod.

In case you don't know, nimrod is a fine word for hunter. According to Webster's Collegiate Dictionary, if the word is capitalized it refers to a descendent of Ham who was represented in the book of Genesis as a mighty hunter and a king of Shinar. I did some bible reading of my own and discovered that Nimrod is the first to be called a hunter, and not just *a* hunter, but a *mighty* hunter before the Lord. To be called nimrod by a fellow sportsman or sportswoman is quite an honor. However, Webster also states that nimrod can be used as slang referring to an "idiot" or "jerk."

As a writer (as well as a hunter), this isn't my first time to take issue with a misused word. Using the word, "nimrod" to refer to a sloppy hunter is similar to cursing. Randy Roth, however, deserves the honor of being named as a mighty hunter. I would even go so far as to say a mighty hunter before the Lord. Not because of any spiritual beliefs Randy might have, but because he truly admires and respects the land and animals he hunts. He is also the most successful hunter I have ever met. Perhaps his admiration and respect have something to do with his success. He never takes a questionable shot, waiting instead until he's convinced of hitting his mark.

"One of the saddest things ever," Randy says, "is to leave a wounded animal in the woods."

Entering his home is like stepping into a museum. The first thing The Cat Man and I see is a towering grizzly, not posed in a stance ready to attack, but rising as a curious giant overlooking his kingdom. Three other bears surround the grizzly, and dozens— yes, I really mean it—dozens of other animals. A cougar cranes his neck to view us. His front paws grip the top of an abandoned wagon wheel. A mountain goat stands on a cliff that seems to be coming right out of the wall. Two pair of antelope are forever locked in a lover's embrace. A red fox is ready to pounce on a tiny unseen critter.

With mouth agape, I walk through the room and wish I had my oil paints with me. These animals appear more alive than dead, and I feel as if I'm wandering through a magical forest. I'm totally amazed to discover that Randy does all his own taxidermy. I know several taxidermists who do a fine job, but none compare to what I'm seeing in Randy's living room. Stacks of antlers remind me of similar piles in Jackson Hole, Wyoming.

An antler chandelier softly lights the room. Shelves beneath the high ceiling spotlight three-tiered rows of bear skulls neatly lined according to size. Mink, elk, caribou, deer—you name it—it's here.

A trip down the long ell-shaped hall reveals Randy's history. He is not only a mighty hunter; he carries the creative power of an artist and has snapped a quality self-photo over every animal he has ever taken. I recognize several of the scenes, and it brings us to the reason I'm here. Randy has promised to share his story of how he took one of the biggest-skulled bears in our neck of the woods. I realize right away that it's going to be hard for me to get the interview with The Cat Man and Randy completely engrossed in swapping stories. I find myself joining in the melee and soon realize that the man is a treasure trove of hunting wisdom. I get out my miniature keyboard and start typing.

"Most people don't spend enough time in the woods," Randy says. "Every skull you see on those shelves represents many hours of tracking, preparation, and patient waiting. I spend a lot of time scouting in the spring to map out where I want to be in the fall. I've discovered most fresh bear tracks when I was hunting for something else. When I find fresh bear sign, I hike back to my pickup, change all my hunting clothes, find a creek to get all the scent off and head back to my spot one hour before dark—bear time."

His wife, Cherri, interrupts, shaking her head. "Whenever I hear Randy say, 'bear time,' I think, 'Oh no! Where are they?'"

Randy tells us that it took him nineteen trips to get Big Skull, his most recent prize. "It's easier to walk in at three or four in the afternoon to set up," he says. "That way, you still have time to back out if the wind changes."

He insists that if the wind changes, you might as well call it a night. He also says that if you don't see fresh bear sign, you might as well go somewhere else. "You put in hours and hours," Randy says, "just hoping for three seconds when a bear will come close enough to harvest."

Finding Big Skull was nearly an accident. Randy had already wasted precious hunting time following tracks in the Applegate unit that turned out to be a sow and two cubs. The next ten days he sat over a narrow grassy draw, but the wind whipped every which way. Finally he headed to the High Cascades and simply stopped in a grassy, forested area to check out where the animals were coming and going.

"I've discovered that bears eat mostly grass in the spring," Randy says. "I found Big Skull's tracks and waited for him four days in a row. On the fourth evening, I got there late and he didn't come through, so I returned in the morning to check the dew for track direction. I was just sitting on a stump when I spotted movement to my right and there he was. I wasn't even planning to hunt, but I had my rifle with me, so I brought him down. That's how it happens sometimes. It's just that simple. Other times, it's like it was in the Applegate Unit for me—you put in lots of miles and waste a lot of fuel and never find a thing."

Randy shares other stories with us as the evening fades away, but The Cat Man and I never look at a clock. Time has slowed as we each relive our special hunting moments. I look up at the grizzly towering above us as Randy encourages me by telling the story of a fishing friend who fished for several years without ever catching a thing. "Then one day, he caught a fish and has been catching them ever since," Randy says.

I listen to Randy's words of wisdom and am grateful that bringing home the big one, or even the little one, is not a prerequisite for sharing in the camaraderie of nimrod. All it takes in our neck of the woods is a willingness to get outside, a curiosity to discover something new, and a listening ear when it's time to relate stories. And stories is what it's all about, because the ability to relive a story is what can never be taken away from us. When the time comes when we can no longer trek the mountain trails, we can be back there in a moment through the telling of a story.

Such is the way of Nimrod.

Bear Track

The Cat Man

Hunting the High Cascades

I DREW A SPECIAL TAG for the High Cascade hunt this season. I have a great camp with a wall tent near a stream deep in the wilderness. I could stay out here for months instead of ten days. My rifle is freshly oiled. My aim is true. I'm eager to nail my first buck.

On opening morning, the Cat Man joins me, and he heads one way and I the other. "See ya at noon," I say.

But I know I won't. We've yet to find each other after setting a designated meeting place and time. It's the wilderness, after all, and neither of us carries a watch. I can tell time by the sun, but I seldom look at the sky when I'm following a good game trail. Doesn't matter. We'll meet back at the tent after sundown and swap stories.

I head for my secret meadow and am exactly where I want to be when the sun rises.

I recently read an article written by John Barsness about still-hunting. He said to take five tentative steps, like a deer, then stand for five minutes, watching. I'm supposed to repeat that action until I see something, and I'm supposed to watch more than I move. I take five steps and stop. I'm overlooking the perfect meadow. There's lots of feed and water and plenty of cover on the perimeter.

One minute passes. Two. Is it really only two? It feels more like ten. The only movement I see is wings of flitting birds. Three minutes pass and I move. I take ten steps to the next tree. They're slow steps. I roll my boot from heel to toe, keeping my weight along the outside of my foot just like Barsness instructed. The weather is hot and dry. Branches crackle beneath my feet, pinecones snap and dry needles crunch, but the slow, rolling steps soften the noise.

I wait. One minute. Two. Three. Then I move six steps. This time I wait the full five minutes. I search every tree and bush. I see a movement and my heart rate quickens, but it's only a squirrel. My fingers are cold to the point of being numb and my toes are beginning to hurt. I take five more steps, then nine, then fifteen.

So much for still-hunting.

I spend the rest of the day, climbing mountains, searching every hollow and crevice for signs of a buck. I see a doe and a spotted fawn. I eat lunch on the shores of Grass Lake while frogs croak out a wilderness song. I find fresh bear sign and smell his heavy scent. I even find tracks of what I am sure must be a big buck, but I never see antlers. By evening my feet feel like heavy blocks of wood. I am not a happy camper.

"You're going about it all wrong," The Cat Man says when I return to camp.

"Obviously," I agree. "But I really want to get a buck. I hunted every single day of deer season last year and never got a shot."

The Cat Man shakes his head. "You don't understand. It's supposed to be fun."

Fun? There was a time when hunting *was* fun to me, but somewhere along the line it changed to an obsession. I want to prove that I'm a "real hunter."

As I sit by the fire, stirring the coals and avoiding the Cat Man's scrutiny, I realize he's right. Statistics show that most hunters are lucky to even see an animal, so if hunting isn't fun, then what am I doing out here?

On Sunday morning we hike to Honeymoon Falls. We carry our rifles, but this is not a serious hunt. This is about putting fun back into the experience. And it works! The cool air is perfect for climbing down into the canyon and back up again. Toward evening, we head out to Boston Bluff.

I choose to sit with my back against a boulder and let the Cat Man do the walking. My hope is that he'll scare something up to me. The breeze caresses my face with the smell of warm huckleberries and incense cedar. I hear a cone start to fall from the top of an enormous cedar next to where I sit. I turn my head to watch and discover that it's not a cone. It's a squirrel that lost its grip and is barreling toward earth!

I watch him tumble twenty feet. Thirty feet. Forty feet! He catches the last branch and swings back and forth like a wayward Christmas ornament not five feet away from me. After a bit, he settles himself and climbs down the trunk of the tree, making his way across the rocks to where I sit. His wet nose touches my jeans before he realizes I'm a person.

He squeals and jumps before scrambling back to the tree and safety.

When the breeze changes direction, I rise to my feet and turn, looking up the bluff. The downhill side gives me a good-sized portion of the forest to overlook. By contrast, the top of the bluff hides most of the uphill from my vision. I should probably move, but a shroud of silence hangs over the forest like it often does just before a storm. I bask in the peace of it, marveling that I have at last learned to enjoy stillness.

When I finally decide to head west, a strange rumbling shakes the ground. The rumbling quickly turns into the sound of pounding feet. A deer rounds the corner at full speed and nearly runs into me. He halts so fast that his hooves skid in the dirt not twenty feet away from me. Little swirls of dust rise up between us. I force myself to take deep, slow breaths.

He's a young buck. Little nubbins stick out of his head where antlers will one day rise in majestic glory. He tilts his head and slowly moves toward me, sniffing the air with his nose like a dog would do. The breeze blows in my favor. I can smell his musky scent, but he can't smell me.

He's almost near enough to figure me out when I hear more pounding feet. The youngster throws a quick glance behind him and leaps down the hill. I raise my rifle. But it's not a buck I see through my scope. It's a huge doe that skids to a stop in the exact place the young buck halted. She doesn't come any closer. She simply stands frozen in that ridiculous position with her stiff front legs spread out like a pair of skinny trees. I keep my rifle raised but my finger well away from the trigger.

We continue to hold our stare down until the doe eventually walks away.

Not long after she leaves, The Cat Man soon joins me. We climb to the top of the bluff where we watch the crimson glow of the setting sun turn Devil's Peak into a blazing pitchfork. Seeing it from this angle and in this light, I can understand how it was named.

I turn full circle. The clouds are piling up over Bunchgrass, and a fluorescent glow highlights the Crater Lake Rim. Mudjekeewis is in shadow and Lake Ivern is black with fast approaching night. The Cat Man and I pull out our flashlights and slowly make our way back to camp. It's been a good day. We did some hiking and some hunting and we had fun. We warm ourselves around the campfire and share the experiences of our day. The Cat Man points out that my skills as an outdoorswoman and hunter have improved.

I bask in his compliment and realize I didn't have to bag an animal in order to gain his admiration. What he likes most is the fact I am out here sharing his love of the outdoors.

The rest of the week goes pretty much the same. It's too bad the moon stays out all night, every night. It's beautiful to look upon, but it gives the deer too much opportunity to feed. Like newborn babies, they sleep all day and eat all night.

I wake up one morning to find deer tracks less than fifteen feet from my bed. From now on, I keep my rifle next to my sleeping bag, ready for the first rays of golden sunlight to reveal a buck, but it never happens. I sneak up on nine different deer throughout the week.

None of them have antlers.

I come home empty-handed once again. But my heart is full of wonder, and I know you've heard this before, but there's always next year.

And next year I won't be so hard on myself. If I get a buck, well, that's great, and you'll hear about it for sure, but if I don't get a buck it's no big deal, because hunting the High Cascades is fun . . . and that's what hunting is all about.

Eric Johnson

Pipe
Dreams

"I ALWAYS WANTED TO LOAD UP A PACK with hunting gear and head back into the wilderness where no man has gone before," our long-time friend David Johnson says, "I could never find anybody to go with me, and I couldn't do it myself, because I couldn't carry all my gear in one trip. I figured it was just a pipe dream, something that would never come about."

It wasn't as if David never had a chance to hunt. He treks the woods with his muzzleloader and keeps the family freezer stocked with venison. But to get back into the woods where he wouldn't see another person . . . now that was a dream. When his 28-year-old son, Eric, shared his own dream with his dad to learn good hunting and wilderness skills, David started making plans.

He picked a rugged destination at 6,000 feet elevation five miles inside the wilderness. Nothing but patchy abandoned trails led through thick timber to a small, uncharted lake. Their gear included an 8x12 tent, a propane lantern, and a two-burner Coleman stove. The father-and-son team figured they could handle the extra weight. David was in his mid fifties at the time, but his six-foot-one frame packed 220 pounds of muscle. Eric stood a formidable six-foot-three and weighed 240 pounds. As a Deputy Sheriff, he seldom needed to ask the same question twice of any prisoner. Both men worked out regularly at a local gym.

They hiked for five-and-a-half hours on Friday afternoon. They lost their way several times and reached the lake after dark. Then they proceeded to assemble a borrowed tent. David read the directions by flashlight while Eric followed his instructions. When the job was completed David said, "We did this all wrong."

Eric raised his eyebrows, "What do you mean, Dad?"

"There wasn't enough bickering and fighting."

The father and son never did argue the entire week they were in the wilderness. They survived bad weather, bad choices of equipment, frigid baths in the lake, and long days of endless hikes without finding any fresh scat or a single elk track. Yet they continued to hunt through sizzling afternoons when the sun cooked the forest with an unusual heat wave, through pouring rain that lasted for an entire day and night, through snow and ice that turned the wilderness into a crunchy wonderland. Yet, they found no elk sign.

On Monday afternoon, after spending the entire morning drying out their wet clothes, father and son headed down the hill below camp. Snow covered the forest with a perfect white blanket. *Too perfect.* They yearned to see the teardrop shapes of hoof prints.

Eric stopped and said, "Dad, there's no elk up here."

David was inclined to agree. He lowered his head and thought: *This looks like it's going to be another of my pipe dreams that doesn't turn out. We got away from the people, and it looks like we got away from the elk too!*

When he raised his head, he discovered a sight that made him change his mind. They had entered a heavily wooded area where huge horn rubs marked several trees. The rubs stretched well over his head. He took a deep breath, inhaling the rich smell of musk. There were no tracks, but David's senses became sharpened and aware. Eric seemed to understand, for he had fallen unusually quiet.

Midafternoon, the two men stopped for lunch. David sat on one log and Eric on another. Neither man spoke as their eyes searched the timber.

The forest remained quiet and still like it often does following the first snow. After lunch, David held the rifle while Eric stuffed his hands into his gloves. David looked past his son and spotted movement—an enormous six-point elk strolling out of the brush.

David placed his hand on Eric's shoulder and pointed down the hill. "There, is a very large bull," he whispered.

Eric raised his eyebrows in disbelief, but he knew enough to look down the hill instead of at his father. His eyes shot wide. He pulled at his gloves, but they resisted, so he yanked them off with his teeth. Then he grabbed the rifle, raised it, and aimed at the bull.

The unsuspecting bull kept his head down and meandered through the brush. As he left one bush and headed for another, David's thoughts raced. All of the talks he had shared with his son about where to shoot an animal; don't be too quick to shoot or you'll make a bad shot; and don't wait too long, either, or the bull will leave you talking to yourself, wondering what went wrong—all of this had come down to the final test.

Eric's window of opportunity was about ten feet wide. He only had three or four seconds to fire.

Come on . . . Come on . . . David swallowed his excitement and said in a quiet voice, accentuating each word, "Take. The. Shot. NOW!"

The much anticipated explosion of Eric's 300 magnum shattered the silence. The bull walked on as if nothing had happened. Eric twisted his mouth into a grimace and turned to his father. "I missed it. I can't believe I missed it."

"Follow me," David whispered. He had seen the bull flinch with the shot. He blew on his cow call as he crept to a better vantage point on the hillside overlooking the brush, then he pointed and said, "Shoot him when he comes out." The words barely left his lips when the bull stepped into the open. BOOM! Hair flew as the 180-grain Hornady found its mark.

The bull raised his head in surprise and looked at the men. Then he turned and hurried downhill. He was moving out at a good pace, but he never once broke into a run. Eric had the rifle raised and ready to shoot again, but David knew better. He gently placed a hand on his son's arm and said, "Don't shoot."

"B-but he's getting away."

"No. He's going down."

In that moment, the bull stumbled and fell.

Father and son approached the massive bull together. Eric stood over the soft tan hide and exclaimed, "He is huge!"

David could neither talk nor swallow. Later, he explained, "I had to brush away tears and thank the gracious God I serve for allowing me to take part in this moment with my son."

Eric hunkered down and discovered that both bullets had found their mark, even though the bull had merely flinched with the first shot. He looked up and said, "You know, Dad, this is kind of sad. This bull has lived so many years and gone through so many winters, and now he's dead." He shook his head. "But I'm not sorry I shot him. No more hard winters. No more starvation." He dropped to his knees and commenced to field dress his first elk.

Getting the elk out of the woods proved to be the major test. Earlier that morning, they had stripped down to fanny packs. Their game bags and most of their gear were back at the tent. Their food and water were gone as well. They each grabbed a horn and pulled on the elk, attempting to drag it out whole. The head tilted to the side, but the body refused to budge. They might as well have tried to move a giant redwood whose roots reached far into the ground.

"This is really heavy," Eric said.

After a brief discussion, they quartered the elk and threaded a seven-foot pole through the hindquarters for easier handling. It took six hours and over sixty trips to cover a third of a mile. They carried the head a short distance then went back for the hindquarters. Next, they returned for the front quarters and then made a fourth trip for the carcass. They repeated the entire process many times, leapfrogging up to the ridge.

Throbbing pain stabbed their backs, cramped their legs, burned their shoulders, and stiffened their necks. Their hands and feet turned into frozen aching stumps. They had no food or water, and it was dark. Eric turned to his father and said, "Well, Dad, we gotta spend the night here."

The huge men attempted to huddle beneath a one-person solar blanket. Soon Eric growled, "Dad, this isn't gonna work."

They gave up trying to sleep. Instead, they found a large hole and placed the meat inside and covered it with the solar blanket. Then, with much chuckling, they relieved themselves in a full circle around the hole. They hoped the human smell would forestall scavengers. Eric lifted the elk head to his shoulders. The eye guards of the antlers were far enough apart that Eric's head fit between them.

"Lead the way to the truck and I'll follow," he said.

There was no moon and the snow had turned to ice. There was absolutely no sign of a trail to follow. So, David struck out cross-country. Whenever David took too much time looking for an easy way through the trees, the tip of a horn poked him in the middle of his back followed by, "Oops, Sorry Dad."

After two hours, David offered to carry the head.

Eric said, "No. When I pulled the trigger, I made a commitment. I'll carry the head all the way."

David walked as fast and hard as he could. The pride he felt for his son kept him close to tears the entire time. The young man never once whimpered or complained as they plodded across the frozen ground for five hours. It was the same the next day when they returned and broke camp. They moved the frozen tent and equipment to the location where their meat was safely kept.

They constructed a new camp, built a roaring fire and proceeded to bone out the meat. It took them the rest of the day and part of the next morning. They filled six large plastic bags with 330 pounds of meat, placed them in the middle of a tarp, and cut two ten-foot poles to make a travois. David took one side and Eric the other, each holding a pole with one arm and locking their other arms for balance. When they came to a log or other obstruction, one of them would pick up the back end and walk it over. They worked all day without any food or water.

When David was tired and ready to give up, Eric was at his strongest. When Eric was becoming weary, David would feel a spurt of energy. They carried each other emotionally throughout the day and ended up at the truck after dark.

Eric dropped everything and grabbed his father in a big bear hug. "Dad, we made it."

"You did great," David said.

Instead of returning home to warm beds, they hiked back into the wilderness to spend the rest of the night in camp. The next morning they broke camp and headed out for the final time.

Once home, Eric proudly filled the family freezer.

"The bull was the icing on the cake," David later told me. "The entire trip was a gift—the humor of seeing my son try to stuff himself into a borrowed sleeping bag that only came to his armpits and the challenge of working together to overcome myriad obstacles. One of my favorite moments was when I was dipping water from the lake and I turned back toward camp. The snow was falling, and Eric stood and warmed himself by a big fire. The tent was in the background. It was so picturesque it brought tears to my eyes. This time it was more than a pipe dream. It was pure ecstasy to share my love of the outdoors with my son."

Eric Johnson

Trapper Camp

The Cat Man and Norman

Night of
No Moon

THERE'S A LOT OF WILD LAND in our neck of the woods, and The Cat Man and I aim to inspect as much of it as possible before our legs give way to old age.

We recently hiked nine miles through the wilderness midst a steady drizzle of rain to discover a marauding bear had torn our tent to shreds. Hopes of warmth and comfort fled as we moved everything important to the only four-by-four dry spot beneath the torn roof.

When Steve Evans arrived with the mules, he just laughed. "Guess you'll have another adventure to write about." But he assured us he would make the long trek back in the next day with either a new tent or a strong tarp big enough to cover the huge holes the bear had ripped across the heavy canvas. It was a spooky night staring at all those claw and teeth marks decorating our tent.

The second night, I heard something sniffing on the other side of the canvas. I sucked in my breath and waited for bear claws to break through. A loud snort erupted, followed by my scream. The Cat Man bolted to his feet with his .44 ready. We both tuned our ears to the snorting and blowing that started at our tent and echoed across the creek, over the meadow, and on up the hill.

"It's that buck I missed earlier," The Cat Man grunted. "He's smelled us and remembers I scared the wits out of him."

We had seen the buck the night before elk season. We had entered a grove of thick new growth when we suddenly heard the sound of thundering hooves. We couldn't pinpoint a direction and soon discovered why as three does sped by every which way.

We caught a blur behind us and turned just before the buck nearly ran us over. It all happened incredibly fast. The Cat Man raised his rifle, but the buck ducked and did an about face as the bullet whizzed right over his back.

Now, as The Cat Man stood before me in our ruined tent, I laughed. "I bet that's the first time that buck has ever been so close to a rifle shot."

Cat shook his head. "He probably thinks we came out here for the sole purpose of scaring him. We sure didn't do much else." Cat crawled back into his sleeping bag and quickly returned to dreamland while I continued to listen to myriad night sounds.

For the next few days we followed tracks across the high desert and down into the deep forested canyons. We usually hunted together but one day, when I was solo hunting, I spotted a bull elk not long before sunset. A five-foot patch of bushy fir trees separated us, so I couldn't place a shot. I watched him for a few minutes before he sniffed me and blasted out of the brush and across the steep canyon. I followed, not thinking about the setting sun or how far away I was getting from camp.

When the shadows grew long, I realized the wapiti had performed his usual ghostly disappearance. I pulled out my GPS, took a reading, set my compass, and plunged ahead. Soon after sunset snow blanketed the ground and fogged my glasses. There was no trail and no moon, so I followed the compass reading straight up the mountain, clawing my way through thick manzanita brush and over huge windfalls. I stopped when my dying flashlight revealed an inky blackness in front of my feet. There was no choice but to leave the straight and narrow to find a way around the abyss.

The snow was falling harder now, so I saved the flashlight for emergencies. A deer jumped out of the darkness in front of me.

My heart about died. I was sure a bear was out there wandering around in the forest with me. When the abyss was safely behind, I took another compass reading. My glasses were so fogged and full of snow, I stuck them in my coat pocket before moving on.

I crawled through more manzanita and sparse timber, knowing that camp should be near. But no welcoming light beamed through the darkness.

No problem, I thought. *I'll just take a look at my map and see where I've gone wrong.*

I reached in my pocket, and you guessed it, no glasses. I peered hard at my map, but I couldn't make anything out. It seemed reasonable to backtrack to find my glasses. That was a mistake. If you can't see to read a map, how can you find a set of eyeglasses in the snow?

I soon realized the impossibility of my situation, so I carved a giant X through the snow and well into the dirt to mark the spot, then I set out in the general direction of camp.

I wasn't sure whether to leap for joy or groan when I saw The Cat Man's flashlight beaming my way. He had given up on waiting and was coming to my rescue, but coming to my rescue in the wilderness is not a sure thing. I had given him a few gray hairs.

"I could have been all right out here after dark," I assured him. "I've got my backpack and all my gear."

"I worry about you hunting alone," he said.

I knew his worry was justified. Sometimes my blood sugar levels drop so low, I don't think well at all. "Can we talk about this in the morning?" I asked.

We made it through the night, but it wasn't a pretty thing when I had to admit that hunting was out of the question until I found my glasses.

"Did you mark the spot on your GPS?"

"Uhhhhh—"

That's when I had to confess, I had totally forgotten about the modern contraption. Feeling compelled to prove my worth, I reminded him about all the oldtimers who didn't have any fancy equipment, and that my own dad was an oldtimer and had taught me well.

"Besides, *you* hardly ever use your GPS," I reminded him. "I bet I can go back to those glasses with no trouble at all. I'll simply use my landmarks like I've used all my life."

The Cat Man shook his head.

I thought about Jack Hollenbeak winding his way out here when he cut in the Pacific Crest Trail, and how Archie McKillip hunted all over the place without a cell phone or a GPS, and how Wayne Marshall drove cattle out here alone when he was fourteen years old.

Fifteen minutes later I felt like one of the oldtimers' crew when I leaned over and retrieved my glasses from a manzanita bush.

Since that night, The Cat Man sticks pretty close. I really don't mind. Even the oldtimers knew when to take a little help from their friends. And a little help may be the very thing to extend my time of discovery in this wonderful wild land. If you haven't been out here yet, you should begin to make a plan. But while making that plan you might want to schedule it before or after the night of no moon. It's always a good thing to place a safety net around the wild land in our neck of the woods.

The Cat Man

Dale Cathcart and The Cat Man

The Buck
Stops Here

The Tale of Two Brothers Hunting

THE CAT MAN'S BABY BROTHER, Dale, has been driving
up from California to hunt with him now for four years. The
past three have pretty much been a walk in the brush, enjoying
the view, learning good hunting skills, getting familiar with
new territory, and gathering needed gear. But this year Dale felt
ready to get a big buck.

Things looked good on their first morning out. The brothers
locked eyes on a buck and followed it. They hunted all morning
until Dale spotted a tree stump looking back at him. Suddenly he
realized it wasn't a tree stump. It was a bear! The first he had ever
seen in the woods. He had no idea whether it was legal or not,
so he whispered like crazy trying to get The Cat Man's attention,
but to no avail. Finally, he just hollered out his brother's name.

But by that time the bear was trotting down the hill and out of sight.

The rest of the day, both men found it difficult to focus on deer when they really wanted to find that bear. They saw nothing but does and lots of bear scat.

The next day proved similar. Both men found their focus fixing on that bear more than deer.

By Tuesday the brothers forced themselves to get back to deer hunting. They chased tracks in the snow until they realized the swirling wind was causing their scent to push the deer further away. They stopped to regroup and discovered they had gotten so caught up in the hunt they had no idea where they were.

The Cat Man said, "I know there's a road over there somewhere, and one over this way, but I have no idea how far or which direction. I don't even know which way we're headed." He laughed and Dale followed with a nervous chuckle. Then both men sat down to eat while waiting for their GPS's to register. There was too much cloud coverage for The Cat Man's older GPS, and Dale's was taking a long time to work.

There they were, with no more food, no matches, and hopelessly lost.

Finally, Dale's GPS registered, and they discovered they were less than twenty feet from the road with thick forest and brush between. The brothers laughed at themselves all the way back to the truck. They spent the rest of the day at a nearby rock pit banging away at targets with an arsenal of guns and sighting in their hunting rifles. The Cat Man's was right on, but Dale's wasn't quite as on as it should have been, a fact that would make a big difference later.

Wednesday was a total loss.

Rain poured from a black sky the entire day. They returned home early, miserable, soaked to their bones, and smelling like wet earth.

The next day was Dale's last to hunt. They hiked through several ravines, ending up in an area cleared of brush. The Cat Man felt too exposed as he climbed to the top of the ridge. So, he turned to Dale and said, "We probably won't see anything in here, but the wind is in our face, so that's a good thing."

As soon as the words left his mouth a doe trotted across the ridge and came within twenty feet. She didn't spook because the wind was good, but when she reached the other side of the exposed forest, she got a whiff and blew out of there.

"Don't move," The Cat Man whispered, "something else is coming."

Sure enough.

A big buck with a wide 4x6 rack hurried down the hill and stopped in front of them. The Cat Man raised his rifle. Dale shot. The buck kept coming, so The Cat Man pulled his trigger. The buck spun and darted off. The Cat Man watched him disappear into the brush below. He was fairly confident his bullet had found its mark, but instead of heading after the buck, he stared at the ground.

"What are you doing?" Dale asked.

"Looking for my brass."

Dale grabbed The Cat Man's brass off the ground, stuck it in front of his face and said, "Let's go!"

The Cat Man stayed where he was and said, "Where's your brass?"

"Forget the brass!" Dale shouted. "Let's get after that buck."

The Cat Man stalled as long as he could, not wanting to move too soon and chase the buck off. His heart sank when he didn't see any blood trail. Finally, when he had just about lost all hope, they spotted a large blood splash. After another search, The Cat Man found the fallen buck.

Both men were excited until they discovered the buck only had one bullet hole in it. Both men shot the same caliber and rifle brand, so it would be hard to know which one missed. Dale figured he probably missed, because his rifle was sighted in at 150 yards and The Cat Man's rifle was right on. But then again… you never know. The Cat Man figured his bullet found the mark, because the hole was right where he aimed, but there was no way to know for sure.

Dale broke into a slow grin. "It's an excellent buck," he said, "I'm willing to share if you are."

"Sounds like a plan," The Cat Man said. Then he gutted the deer, leaving it whole instead of quartering it because he knew I wanted photos. The brothers drug the buck across five ravines, slipping down into and climbing up out of each, dreaming about sleds, helicopters, and some kind of four-wheel contraption, anything to make their job easier. The buck started out weighing about 190 pounds, but felt more like 1400 pounds at the end of their trek.

Later, while the buck hung in the shed and the aches and pains fell away, Dale said it was a fun experience and that he was looking forward to next year. "With any luck," he said to The Cat Man, "we'll be able to do this again." Then he grinned and said, "And you'll be able to get your own buck. Ha ha ha ha ha ha ha ha."

For the record, the buck belongs to *both* brothers. Since The Cat Man is getting the head mounted, we offered to share, six months at our house, six months at Dale's. Dale called his wife and she nixed the idea; only Tiffany lanterns hang in her hallway. She also only wanted two of the 42 pints of venison we canned. Though she appreciates our love of the outdoors, she has a limit.

To this day, whenever we get together, a friendly argument breaks out about who actually shot the buck. So, when all is said and done, the buck stops here, but the story of how the buck stopped drones on and on.

The Cat Man and Dale

Ron Botsford

Christmas
Bull

THE CAT MAN AND I faced the beginning of this year with an empty freezer and a renewed determination to fill it come hunting season. But as The Cat Man guided two return hunter brothers, Ron and Ken Wolff, during the first week of bow season, his hope wavered. He found old sign and precious few tracks. We camped near a stream and found plenty of water and feed. The aroma of ripe huckleberries and warm grass should have lured the wapiti from the dryness experienced by most of the wilderness during the extreme fire danger. But it didn't.

We caught fish in the high mountain lakes, the biggest being a 21-inch Brookie. I picked huckleberries and served them fresh with hotcakes every morning. We showered in the frigid waters of a nearby waterfall. We hiked up, over, down and around. But no elk. Ron had a special encounter with a furry little critter who climbed the log where he was sitting. The critter eye-balled him, wondering at this strange interruption. Ron later discovered he had watched a rare display from a pine martin, but still, no elk.

After ten days of traversing the incredibly rough terrain of steep mountains and thick brush and sneaking around high plush meadows and hidden valleys, we left discouraged and depressed.

It was the first time The Cat Man had left the woods without seeing an elk. "Time to hang up my hat," he said. It was just an expression. What he really meant was that he thought his days as a guide were over.

"It's just one season," I said. "Every guide has to have at least one bad one." But the encouragement fell on deaf ears. It wasn't till later, when the Cat Man talked with his bow hunter friend, Ron Botsford, that he began to see light at the end of the tunnel.

"And this time it's not an oncoming train," Cat said.

It seems that Ron had the same experience as The Cat Man. It's not so much that misery loves company, but Ron held the reputation of a successful elk hunter. If he didn't see elk in the same area, then perhaps The Cat Man was right. Perhaps there were no elk to be had this year. But unlike Ron, we didn't have the option of moving our camp.

"I covered fifteen miles and stepped through two inches of snow as I circled McKie Camp," Ron says. There wasn't an elk track in the whole place. There was a cow and a calf heading down toward Solace and that was it."

The Cat Man had seen the tracks of the same cow and calf.

Like Cat, Ron felt more disgusted than in any previous year's hunting. He figured the elusive wapiti had to be out there someplace, but there was a lot of "out there" to cover. He turned to Mike, his partner, and said, "I know where to find some elk."

The two men hiked back out of the wilderness and made plans to meet the next day. "We'll head up the road from my house," Ron said. "There's plenty of elk up there."

That's when the fun began. Ron heard elk on the hillside below him as the herd crashed through the brush and snapped branches. He pulled out his bugle and blew. A bull answered from right underneath him. Ron held his breath and stood still as the stone beneath his feet. The drum of his heart pulsed in his ears.

The bull bugled again, a long, haunting sound echoing across the rocky hillside. Ron knew he was in a bad position to take a bull on that steep terrain. His chief aim was to retrieve his partner and out-think the bull, pull the animal into a better position.

71

His plan was to beat the high odds of leaving a bull wounded in the woods with an arrow in its side.

He sneaked through the forest beneath a covering of Manzanita brush, oak and pine trees, slowly moving from one tree to another, stopping at each to get a closer look. Finally, he made it to his partner. Together, they climbed a mile up the steep slope to a rocky ridge.

There, the men discussed which way to go. They figured the elk could always go left or right, or up, or wherever they decided they wanted to go. It would be a gamble either way.

Up seemed the logical direction, so Ron pulled out his bugle for the second time and blew.

Nothing.

Was it an eternity or a few seconds? The hillside lay in a cloak of utter silence. Ron feared he had miscalculated. Perhaps the elk had chosen to go down instead of up. Then suddenly he heard the sound of cracking branches and movement down the ridge. He squatted and peered through the brush until he picked out an ear, a part of a tan body, a white rump, a set of antlers.

The bull lifted his head and answered Ron's bugle with one of his own. Then he turned and pulled at the bark of a tree, showing disinterest in the owner of the other bugle.

Ron sneaked up the hill and bugled again. This time, the bull picked up his head and followed. Ron and Mike set up the perfect ambush. The bull had to walk by one man or the other. Ron knocked his arrow and waited. When the bull was twenty-five yards out, he let go. The arrow found its mark in a perfect double-lung shot. The haunting silence was at last broken with a loud, triumphant whoop of joy. "Yeeeeeehaaaaw!"

The thrill was as great as the first elk I dropped over thirty years ago," Ron says.

The Cat Man took hope from Ron's story and set out on his own to fill our freezer. He hunted one spot, then another, not seeing any elk but seeing plenty of sign. He stepped behind a tree, pulled out his cow elk call, and gently mewed. His long-time hunting partner, David Johnson, sat on the ground with his back against a stump and his rifle across his lap. After tromping the woods all day and not seeing any wapiti, he didn't expect anything to happen. When a young bull stepped out of the brush not thirty feet away from him, Dave could do little more than stare.

"He was so close, I would have scared him off if I had tried to raise my muzzleloader," Dave told me later.

When the bull sauntered off, Dave looked apologetically at The

Cat Man. Cat just smiled and raised the call back to his lips. Eeeeyow. Eeeeyow. Dave raised his muzzle loader and the bull returned. A clean shot and a full freezer.

"That's our Christmas bull," I announced later as I offered our family roasted venison for our holiday meal. But the best present was when The Cat Man walked to the door and grabbed his hat.

"Wanna take a walk?" he said.

"Sure," I answered, grabbing my coat. The thrill is still strong after years of following wapiti. I joined my own husband for a walk through the woods with the renewed hope of many more years ahead of us.

An elkless wood might get a good hunter down for a short while but not for the count.

Sandy and Cat at Trapper

Walt Wingler

A Year to Remember

YOU PROBABLY KNOW THE FEELING...the last day of hunting season and you get a little desperate. Rack size no longer matters; you simply hope to see *something* that qualifies for your tag. Walt Wingler was in just such a position last fall when he was hunting elk with his muzzleloader.

The elusive animals had evaded him all week and now he was down to the last day. He had seen a beautiful buck, with a rack size and symmetry that would have done any hunter proud. Today he had seen another buck he would have settled for if it had been deer season, but the wapiti seemed to have turned into ghosts leaving no sign they were anywhere near.

The weather was perfect for tracking, plenty of snow, yet not so deep as to be a hindrance, and clouds dropped so low to the ground the atmosphere was almost spiritual. His heart started to race when he discovered the tracks of two wapiti leading up the mountain.

Finally, he had a chance to fill his tag.

At the top of the mountain, the tracks led into a canyon so deep and dark it would take a month to pull out a downed elk. Walt wisely turned away. By now, he just hoped to see any kind of living animal out there, something to let him know he wasn't alone in his white world. Then he spotted fresh cougar tracks... not just one set, but two!

Picking up his pace, he followed the tracks down the skid road. When they dove off the side, he followed through the brush and trees.

"I thought it was a good opportunity to see just how fresh those tracks were," Walt says. I had a bit of reservation following two predators since I didn't have a sidearm, but it was just so darn exciting finding something alive out there. Besides, I had been hunting all my life, was confident with my shooting skills, and knew I could reload in a timely manner."

Walt followed the tracks until they were so crisp and clear he was certain the animals had to be nearby. He set up beside a large cedar tree where he could see about 35 yards in the direction the cats were headed. That's about as far as he could see in any direction because of brush, downed logs, and trees. Then he pulled out a varmint call and offered his best rendition of a traumatized and dying rabbit. He had tried this call before with not much success, but he figured it was worth a try to see what would happen.

He was down on his knees, whipping on the call like a mad harmonica musician when he saw a flash of fur about 30 years in front of him.

"Oh sh—. Here we go," Walt said. The cougar was running straight toward him.

Walt already had his muzzleloader to his shoulder when the cat leaped over a large log. His impressive tail followed like a long line of train cars. The cat landed behind a leafless bush and slowly started quartering toward Walt who had the bead of his 50 caliber muzzleloader aimed just behind the cat's front shoulder. At fifteen yards, Walt dropped the hammer.

The cat went straight up in the air, did a big flip and, as soon as it hit the ground, it was gone. With the smell of gunpowder still in the air, Walt immediately reached for his powder.

"All I could think was, *Reload. Reload. Reload,*" Walt says.

He put a patch and ball in the barrel and rammed it home. Then he got out a capper and was attaching it to the nipple when he caught a glimpse of something to the left. What he saw made his heart take a flying leap.

The other cat was starting to crouch and was staring straight at Walt, sizing him up for lunch.

Still on his knees, Walt finished attaching the cap and pulled the muzzleloader up to his shoulder. Looking down the barrel, all he could see was a portion of the cat's head and ears behind a bush, but the main thing that caused his adrenalin to rise threefold was a pair of intense cat eyes staring straight back at him.

Already approaching the point of sheer terror, Walt heard another noise coming from behind.

"This is the moment when all your training shifts into gear," Walt says. "I wanted to look behind me and see if the wounded cougar was closing in, but at the same time, I didn't want to lose eye contact with the crouching cougar. He knew I was there and had seen me move, but he still wasn't going anywhere. I only had one shot and it better be well-placed or I would be the one for dinner."

Walt stole a frantic glance behind him. Seeing no immediate danger from that direction, he scooted to the left for a better shot at the crouching cougar. He told himself to not let adrenalin get to him or he wouldn't be able to hold still enough to shoot. After a calming breath, he touched the trigger. Through the cloud of smoke, he saw the cougar jump and disappear into the brush.

Reload. Reload. Reload, Walt told himself again, and by the time he was ready to fire, both cats had disappeared at the brush line.

Oh shhh—, he thought. Now I've got two wounded cougars in the brush I have to go find. Heart still thumping hard and knowing he had placed his shot well on the first cat, Walt followed the first cat's blood trail while keeping his eyes peeled for the second. With a thick canopy overhead and bare ground and patches of snow beneath his feet, Walt tracked the cat fairly easily and found him about 150 yards downhill piled up in a bush. But pulling him up that steep grade was another matter.

The snow was wet and slick, and the hill was as steep as a cow's face. Walt had to hold onto tree branches in order to pull the 140-pound cat back up to the road. At one point, he had to pull the animal over the same log he had seen it jump nearly two hours before.

After loading the cat onto the back of his pickup, Walt turned back into the forest to look for the second cat. He was pleased to discover that his shot had plowed through a stump immediately in front of where the cat had crouched. Tracking the cat for a while, he saw that all four paws had landed about every ten feet heading down to where Walt had made a clean shot on the other cat. He had no doubt that the second cougar was no worse for wear.

As a storm picked up and wind started to blow, Walt relaxed knowing he hadn't left a wounded animal in the woods. All in all, it was a very good year. No elk . . . but a bear, a buck, a tom turkey, and a cougar.

"Next year," Walt says, "I'm taking it easy. I'm gonna hunt just as hard and have fun, but this was my year. You just don't forget these things."

Cougar Country

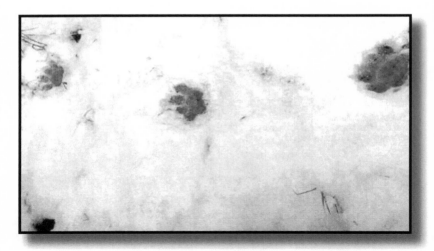

Cat Tracks

Sandy Cathcart

Tresa Finchum

The Day the Skies
Fell Silent

ONE OF MY FAVORITE HUNTING SPOTS is deep in the middle of the Sky Lakes Wilderness, and that's where I was when terrorists attacked New York City on September 11, 2001.

You might think the attack on The World Trade Center wouldn't affect us much in our neck of the woods. After all, New York City is three thousand miles away on the other side of the U.S. Many of the people who fill its streets live in skyscrapers, and most have never experienced a life of living off the land. On the contrary, we're mountain folk. We spend much of our time in the wilderness, and we seldom sit in front of a television.

If you had walked with me on September 12, you might have been surprised to follow me up the winding switchbacks of Gopher Ridge while I searched for a high place to use my cell phone. It wasn't the noise of sirens or the blast of explosions that alerted me to a feeling of wrongness. It was the uncanny utter silence of the skies. For an entire day and night only one plane had flown over our section of the wilderness, a C-130 tanker carrying a load of retardant toward a forest fire.

The rumble of that single plane caught my full attention. In the shroud of silence following I realized what had been missing. The night before, as I sprawled in my sleeping bag beneath the stars, I had seen no blinking red and green lights making tracks across the heavens. Usually, I can count several in a short span of time.

The silence made me think of oldtimer, Jack Hollenbeak. He traveled these woods before the noise of airplanes echoed through the forest. Tuesday, September 11, was the first time in my life I had ever experienced what Jack had taken for granted.

Instead of the joy I expected to find, I felt an urge to make contact with the outside world, an unusual desire since my whole purpose in entering the wilderness was to get away from the noise and busyness of the world.

I grabbed my backpack and started up the switchbacks, one foot in front of the other. When the sun was high in the sky, I phoned the Cat Man.

"America is under attack," he said.

His words made no sense to me and it took a full minute to find a response.

I sat on a high plateau with the breeze changing the color of the tall grass from green to gold and back again. I heard the drone of bees and a dozen different kinds of small insects as they darted around scarlet paintbrush, purple larkspur, mountain bluebells, and golden asters. Black hooded Oregon Juncos beeped and babbled in the trees. The sweet smell of chokecherries and wildflowers mingled with the aroma of warm fir trees, a combination of Christmas and summer all rolled together. Storm clouds gathered in the eastern sky with a hint of winter on its way. A hawk soared freely in the air above me. And all the while silence mantled the earth. How could it be possible among all this stillness that America was under attack?

"Attack?" I asked.

The Cat Man told me of the hijacking and the thousands of people who were feared dead. "It's worse than Pearl Harbor," he said.

I watched a doe feeding beneath tall timber behind me. Ants crawled at my feet. They had no idea of the terror humans could inflict on one another. They simply lived one day at a time in search of necessary food and shelter. The battery of my cell phone went dead before I discovered all the details of the hijacking. I considered walking off the mountain across the three miles of remote trails to my Jeep Cherokee. It didn't seem right that I should enjoy this incredible peace while so much of the world suffered. But the Cat Man had urged me to stay saying, "You can do as much there as you can down here. The president is calling for everyone to pray."

I rose to my feet and started the trek across the mountain. My feet felt incredibly heavy as I sank back into the depths of the wilderness.

As I walked, I joined my country in prayer. I prayed for the people who had lost so many loved ones in the attacks. I prayed for our leaders to have wisdom in knowing how to retaliate against such evil. I prayed for protection for my family and friends. And as I prayed, I bawled my eyes out. The skies left their silence and joined me in a terrible display of thunder and lightning, rain and hail. It was as if the heavens themselves were weeping.

I thought the world had never seen such evil. Then I remembered that oldtimer Jack Hollenbeak had lived through two world wars.

Evil has been around a long time.

As I hiked back into the wilderness I caught a small glimpse of that evil in my own heart, in the way of unkind thoughts about others, and I took a vow that I would do all in my power to withstand any root of bitterness, or seed of hate, or anger to develop in any way in my own life. No longer would I allow myself to indulge in road rage, or shouting matches or even negative talk about one of my fellow humans. And I prayed that if I failed in my vow, God would grip my heart at the first sign of evil and fill me with remorse and the power to turn around midstream and do what is right. It might not seem like a big thing, but it is the beginning of the making of a hero.

We are a nation of heroes, unsung individuals who share a common love of freedom and who will drop everything to help one another in a time of crises. We've seen this example in the response of people in far-off New York City in their hour of attack, and we've seen it here, in our neck of the woods, year after year, through the timberfallers, truck drivers, mill workers, hunters, quilt makers, berry pickers, and myriad mountain folk who have always helped one another in a time of need.

Heroes are simply people who care about each another, and that's what America is all about. But more than that, we have also seen that the entire world is full of heroes, many of whom stepped up to help us in our hour of need. As we approach Thanksgiving Day and the New Year, may we all aspire to be the heroes who will make a difference for better in our world.

Challenging Wapiti

The Makings
of a
Successful Hunt

MOST PEOPLE ENTERTAIN THE IDEA that any hunter worth his soup is going to return from a hunting trip with a freezer full of meat in the back of his truck. That idea is a fantasy born of misunderstanding and a lack of information.

The truth is, most hunters will be fortunate to even see an animal. The Oregon Big Game Regulations lists the 1996 success rate for hunters of Rocky Mountain Elk to be 22.3 percent. That means 77.7 out of 100 hunters came home empty handed. That's a fairly medium statistic, with bow hunters even less successful. 87.7 Percent of bowhunters left the woods with nothing to show for their trip.

Let's take 100 rifle hunters and 100 bow hunters. Out of the 200 total you have at least 34 hunters who stand tall and proud and 165 losers.

Whoa! Wait a minute. Is it really true that those 165 hunters are losers?

That brings up the question—What makes a successful hunt?

I've asked that question of many men and women. To my surprise, I found that a good portion of hunters don't even care if they bring home an animal. Success to them is being out in the woods, enjoying the sights and smells and peace of the wilderness, finding tracks and following sign.

What surprised me even more is that many hunters don't even shoot when they follow sign right up to the animal. They consider it success enough to be able to track down and find their quarry and to learn they had the skills necessary if they really needed the meat.

I came home totally discouraged from my first hunt two years ago. I had practiced shooting for months and honed my skills until I was reasonably sure I could drop a bull with little pain. I scouted the hills and followed herds, snapping hundreds of photos. I crawled over logs and made myself run nine miles three times a week to be in good condition when my big moment came. But it never happened. I never once got to shoot my rifle and missed experiencing the joy of watching the herd. After an entire week in the wilderness, I only saw one wapiti—and that was a cow.

My discouragement was born out of ignorance. I thought The Cat Man would be ashamed of me for coming home empty handed. Instead, he shocked me by saying what I had experienced was more the normal thing and most hunters would be lucky to even see an elk.

He taught me about the reality of a successful hunt.

It's standing with the wind in your face while listening to every sound, honing into the tiniest of noises—the rustling of leaves, the scrape of a hoof, the swoop of a crow's wings, the song of falling fir pods. It's being able to find fresh tracks and follow sign—picking out recent rubs and finding bits of an elk's feast of mushrooms. It's squatting down and spotting the flicker of an ear or tail, the outline of a tan rump. It's climbing through falling snow and experiencing an awesome, perfect stillness unbroken by the constant hum of automobiles or human noise. It's sitting at elk camp with frozen fingers lifted toward the flickering flames of the campfire and laughing at the enhanced versions of twice-told stories. It's learning new skills year-round and the hope of next year's camp.

I took the Cat Man's lesson and enjoyed my second season much more than my first. I saw the humor in plodding through waist-deep snow on opening day even though the thick, wet stuff made the possibility of finding a Wapiti almost nil.

When the sun poked through the clouds long enough to turn the mountain into a glistening wonderland, I forgot all thoughts of following elk as I marveled at the stillness before me. I scouted with different hunters, learning new ways of calling the wapiti and using all five senses to discover their whereabouts. I used my compass when hunting alone and never once got lost.

When Andre' Legrand nailed his first bull, the excitement caught me as much as if I had gotten my own.

The big game statistics listed me as a loser, but in the Cat Man's eyes I had experienced a successful hunt.

This year was a bad year for the Cat Man. He didn't pull a muzzle loader tag for himself and guided an older man through general season in an area that really needed to be walked more than the man was able. Yet, neither came home sad.

"You can't believe the amount of food we ate," says Cat. "The food alone would have been good enough reason to be out there."

After two days at a spike camp gagging down something akin to c-rations, one man nearly ran down the hill to get to the good food at base camp. There, they feasted on bear and moose roasts, elk liver, pork ribs, shrimp and crab.

They shared evenings with other hunters around a roaring campfire telling stories of the big ones from earlier years and sightings of cows through the underbrush, as well as swapping expertise to help one another. There's something special about elk camp camaraderie—fathers and sons, husbands and wives, good friends—all share in a common love of the wilderness. The success of one excites the rest of the camp.

"I didn't get one this year," a friend said to me, "But my son got his first elk and that was better than anything I could have done myself."

I learned that fact at last year's Crazy Cayuse Elk Camp.

Another thing I've learned is that hunters make a lot of discoveries while they're out in the woods. It was a hunter who first came upon the Dead Indian Soda Springs way back in 1870 and another hunter stumbled across the northernmost cypress tree right up the hill from my house. Hunters have discovered unknown creeks and lakes, named mountains and outcroppings and have returned home with tales of wildlife doing unusual things.

Some hunters rely on their eyesight, others on their ears; some hike for hours while others sit and wait; yet all find the wilderness a beautiful setting for an enchanting adventure.

So, what of our question? What makes a successful hunt?

If what I'm hearing is true, the only bad hunt is the one in which a buddy is injured or killed. For the number of hunters traipsing through the woods, the safety ratio is in your favor. In other words, by applying good safety measures and honing learned skills, exactly 100 out of 100 hunters can experience a successful hunting trip. With these kinds of odds, it's a good time to take to the woods!

Thank You!

THANKS TO ALL the wild men and women who participated in the stories of this book. You are the heart of the Wild West! I'm so thankful to have been a part of your lives and to have had you be a part of mine.

For those of us who are finding it more difficult to get into our favorite wild places, I hope the reading of these stories will stir up memories so strong that you can smell the scent of a rain-drenched forest and hear the call of coyotes.

Wild is more than a physical untamed place, it's an unrestrained soul soaring on the wings of the wind; it's a connection to our wild Creator.

Thanks to the following who shared stories and wisdom, either in person or through writing! (In no particular order.)

Cat Cathcart	Mike Severini	Ron Wolff
Steve Evans	Eddie LaFerriere	Wayne Marshall
Cristi Rein	Isabella Bird	Dale Cathcart
Nelson Nye	Jim Nugent	Ron Botsford
Archie McKillip	John Barsness	Andre' Lagrand
Jack Hollenbeak	David Johnson	Walt Wingler
Randy Roth	Eric Johnson	Robert Garcia
Marvin Wright	Ken Wolff	Tresa Finchum

Annotations

1. New Breed of Mountain Men *(Oregon Fish & Wildlife Journal,* Winter 2008)

2. The Cat Man Gets His Cat *(Oregon Fish & Wildlife Journal,* Winter 2007)

3. Running With The Herd *(Bugle,* Fall, 1996)

4. In The Company of Nimrod *(Oregon Fish & Wildlife Journal,* Fall 2004)

5. Hunting The High Cascades *(Oregon Fish & Wildlife Journal,* January/February 2002)

6. Pipe Dreams *(Oregon Fish & Wildlife Journal,* March/April 2002)

7. Night of No Moon *(Oregon Fish & Wildlife Journal,* Winter 2005)

8. The Buck Stops Here *(Oregon Fish & Wildlife Journal,* Winter 2009)

9. Christmas Bull *(Oregon Fish & Wildlife Journal,* November/December 2000)

10. A Year to Remember *(Oregon Fish & Wildlife Journal,* Spring 2001)

11. The Day The Skies Fell Silent *(Oregon Fish & Wildlife Journal,* November/December 2002)

12. The Makings of a Successful Hunt *(Oregon Fish & Wildlife Journal,* January/February 1998)

Contact

SANDY CATHCART is a freelance writer, photographer and artist, as well as a scribe for Restoring The Heart Ministries. She lives in the High Cascades of Southern Oregon with her husband, The Cat Man, where she writes about Creator and everything wild.

Sandy loves hearing from her readers.
You can find her on Facebook:

https://www.facebook.com/sandycathcartauthor/

You can also email her at:

sandycathcart@gmail.com

Request

Reviews are like gold to authors.
If you have enjoyed reading this book
would you please consider leaving a review
at Amazon or Goodreads
and tell your friends about it!

Thanks very much!

Visit

www.needlerockpress.com
for future books!

www.sandycathcart.com
for Sandy's Art & Photography

www.capturingstory.com
for Help with your Writing Project

www.restoringtheheart.com
for Native American Insight

www.ghostdancershadley.com
for Daily Inspiration

Would you like to be on Sandy's mailing list
for future books and notice of upcoming appearances?
email her at:

sandycathcart@gmail.com

What People Are Saying About Needle Rock Press Books

Praise for *Wild Woman: A Daughter's Search For A Father's Love*

From an Oregon Reader

"This book made me do something I don't believe I've ever done with a book before. When I finished it, I immediately went back to the beginning and started reading it again. And found new gems of wisdom the second time."

From an Amazon Reader

"How many times does the enemy of our soul whisper lies into the silence of our minds about those we love or care for? Lies that are born of misunderstandings brought on by imaginings of what we "think" our loved ones say or don't say. How many wasted hours, days or years are spent in anger over words said in a moment of exhaustion, frustration, or disappointment?

"Sandy's story is a beautiful example of what our Creator and Redeemer longs to do in each of us through forgiveness and love. When we allow him to do that in us, we suddenly become free to be loved and to give love, as he heals our broken hearts and restores to us lost relationship."

From an Amazon Reader

"This is a woman who loves the wilderness and is at home in it. She brings you the scents of campfires and forest earth, and the love of the God she calls Creator Redeemer."

Praise for *Shaman's Fire (a novel)*

From an Amazon Reader

"Wonderful book! I couldn't put it down. Written with a clear passion for Native American Culture and spirituality. In this story I found my own memories. It reminded me of so many teachings passed down to me. This book exceeded all my expectations. Keeping me riveted from page one; with complex characters and extraordinary care with details. I highly recommend it!"

From a Goodreads Review

"I did love this book! I have been a reader of varied subjects since a child but have always held a special affection for historical fiction of all genre. The Native history and culture of Southern Oregon is seldom touched by other authors. It was very nice to visit this world filled with insight that was written with the authority of the tribes portrayed.

"The mix of modern day and history keep the pace moving. A good suspense that made me want to know more as I turned the last page. The love story and family conflicts were realistic in their feelings. This was the first work of fiction I have ever read that explains the Great Creator of the North American Indigenous People as the same God that the Europeans brought with them."

From an Amazon Reader

"I loved this book for many reasons. The characters are well-developed. I enjoyed how each chapter was written from a different character's point of view. I thought it was a powerful story of the spiritual warfare of which we are very often unaware. I appreciated the way the author described native traditions, dress and speech . . . I look forward to reading more from this author."

Praise for *Eagle People Journal*

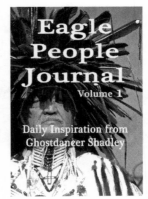

From Julie, an Amazon Reader
"Great food to nourish the spirit!!! A daily reading for each day of the year with a biblical reference should one choose to study further into the promises of our Creator. I can't wait for Volume II."

From Randy, an Amazon Reader
"This is a Christian journal/devotional that encourages, inspires and makes you think more deeply about things. And at the end of every entry, there is a scripture verse from the Bible(God's Word) to read, that seemed to have inspired the entry itself. The devotionals entry's specifically, are beautifully written and told in a Native American way. The book is also very well done, and easy to read."

From Joan, an Amazon Reader
"Ghostdancer Shadley touches your heart with daily words of inspiration on every level. Enlightenment at its best. This book is a must have for daily inspiration. A year's worth of daily reflection on a very spiritual level. The bible verse given at the end of each excerpt, gives an added lesson to be applied. Regardless of your religious background, this book is interpreted for anyone. After reading once, you will return to a special verse where the meaning becomes more powerful. A very good handbook to have for your daily inspiration."

Praise for *Song in the Night*

From an Amazon Reader

"Do not be fooled by the small size of this book. This book literally speaks volumes to women and men who are trying to live in life's inhospitable society. She and her husband take their family outside of that circle to try to raise their family and preserve their own love and beliefs. As a storyteller, Cathcart puts you beside her either struggling with her every muddy footstep or singing a child to sleep. She shares her fears and joys as a wife and mother, living in a world without running water or electricity, that you know instinctively is organic in nature.

Her songs (poetry) are a gift. Her tale so pertinent today in the life of families trying to respond to the world as they seek truth and the higher power. To what extreme do we have to go?

I encourage people take time to share Cathcart's memories of a life few of us are brave enough to set in motion. The personal struggle of faith is well told as it unfolds in relation to the existence of daily living Cathcart style.

Buy the book, settle down, and let Sandy tell you, in her humorous way, how some of her most tragic days and profound joys shaped her and her family's lives forever."

From Chad McComas, Editor of The Christian Journal

"Sandy's book is a wonderful adventure of how God finds us when we need it most and rebuilds our lives. As Sandy shares from her heart and soul all that God did for her you have to wonder if one person could have so many wild adventures and create such an amazing attitude through it all. The book is hard to put down and you feel so honored to share Sandy's life with her."

Made in the USA
Middletown, DE
27 July 2024

58031255R00068